How to Plan an Itinerary for a Spontaneous Adventure:

Volume X of
The Travels of
Senator & Wendy V

- © 2023 by Wendy V. All rights reserved. No part of this publication may be reproduced or transmitted in any form or by any means, electronic or mechanical, including photocopy, recording, or any information storage and retrieval system, without the prior written consent of the author and/or publisher.

- Cover photography © 2023 by David Zuchowski Cover design © 2023 by Wendy V.

ISBN: 979-8-218-19431-4

Other Titles by Wendy V

Travelogues:
How to Read a Compass in the Dark (2006)

How to Change a Flat on a Unicycle (2007)

How to Start a Fire Under the Sea (2009)

How to Eat a Pizza From a Can (2011)

How to Hitch a Ride With No Thumbs (2013)

How to Draw a Map of the Forest (2015)

How to Book a Flight for Last Year (2017)

How to Take a Drink From a Cactus (2019)

How to Set a Clock at the North Pole (2021)

Poetry:
Eventually, Finally (2007)

for my mom,
who never said "No" to the Road

"I don't know how it is I seem to be always writing about myself. I mean all the time to write about other people, and I try to think about myself as little as possible, and I am sure, when I find myself coming into the story again, I am really vexed and say, "Dear, dear, you tiresome little creature, I wish you wouldn't!" but it is all of no use. I hope any one who may read what I write will understand that if these pages contain a great deal about me, I can only suppose it must be because I have really something to do with them and can't be kept out."

~Esther Summerson
Bleak House

Table of Contents

Introduction					i

If At First You Don't Secede...			1

Afterword					45

Author's Note

By now, you should know the drill. If not, just out of curiosity, why are you starting with the tenth volume?

Introduction

I did not set out to write a ten-volume travel series. My initial thought ran something along the lines of *wouldn't it be nice to jot down what we did on our first excursion together?* Several times I had relished reading my grandma's travelogue from a magnificent trip to Europe she and my papa had taken in the early 1970s. Maybe Senator would appreciate such a memento. Grandma's was typed, on a real clickety-clack typewriter; mine would be even simpler-- handwritten in a lovely velvet-covered journal I had picked up on clearance at the bookstore where Senator and I worked and met.

When I told my boyfriend my idea, he deemed it worthy of independently publishing. I had never even considered that possibility. As someone who had plenty of experience creating, engineering, and producing his own music, I now realize that he either wanted me to share in the satisfaction of accomplishing one's own project, or the maddening angst of working through the challenge. Either way, I took his advice, using a company recommended by a friend. I staged a photo for the cover, and Senator was my photographer (for that and many of the subsequent books).

As we continued to spend time together, we continued to travel. It only made sense that I continued to document it. Within about a decade we had reached all fifty states. A few years later we checked off all of the Canadian provinces. (No, I don't care about the territories, so do not email me about the splendors of the Northern Mariana Islands or Nunavut.) Every other June a new book came out, released on the anniversary of our first date. Somewhere along the way I also privately published Grandma's Europe memoir.

Now I come to number ten, which seems a logical place to conclude the series. It's a nice round number, taking us through twenty years together. If you're still reading, I can tell you the significance to this score of years. During the spring of 2003 Senator and I were becoming fast friends. We had in-depth conversations balanced with a common bizarre sense of humor, all converging at a time when we were both in serious need of laughter. I appreciated his wisdom, but I assumed he was mostly just being kind to a younger, dumber coworker. Thus, having no idea we would end up pursuing a life together, I ended a particularly profound conversation session by telling him, "You know, if someday, in twenty years, I run into you, I hope life will have gone really well for you. I mean it..." And I sincerely did. In fact, with the exception of very close family and friends, I had never felt so strongly interested in someone's happiness, success, and well-being. I sort of surprised myself as I said it. I wasn't intentionally planning to drift apart; I just assumed it would be natural and inevitable. Senator has since (many times) informed me that he was none too pleased with my remark that day, wondering why I believed only coincidence would place us in each other's paths in the ensuing years. This is one of the best things he has ever told me. Now twenty years *have* gone by, and I *do* hope things have gone really well for him. (Perhaps you can ask him.)

~Wendy V
April 2023

Chapter 1 (and Only)
If At First You Don't Secede... :
Early April 2023

Note: All related facts in the following chapter are attributed to and verified within the United States National Park Service visitor centers, The Powder Magazine, the Old Slave Mart, and Boone Hall Plantation.

No, we hadn't fallen off the planet since our last trip almost three years earlier. In the first year of the Great Plandemic* many factors pointed us toward the decision to stay close to home. There were so many closures and restrictions that it would have been a waste of time and money to visit places we had anticipated studying, only to miss out on indoor visitor centers, museums, and historic homes that were closed. Accommodations were cutting out breakfasts while maintaining the same rates. Just as annoying, many locations were also insisting visitors wear masks. The only time I would participate in this physically

---

* originally known as "15 Days to Slow the Spread"

and psychologically unhealthy foolishness was 1.)when my job required it in order to earn a living, and 2.)when I had to play the game in some medical facilities.

Perhaps we could have only visited freedom-loving destinations, like when we took a weekend in Tennessee.* True, but a week after returning from there, just as we were contemplating possible summer options, various cities became dangerous riotous shitholes (or shit*tier* holes, as in the case of Chicago), thanks to Antifa and Black Lives Matter. The media basked in the chaos, working hard to pit people against one another, twisting narratives with the ultimate goal of moving us closer to Marxist principles. Unfortunately, many people took the bait and joined the fray. When we had to spend a mostly-sleepless night monitoring live streams of riots, after quickly planning a safe evacuation of my grandma from her home, it was a unanimous decision not to travel for a while.

Seeing the state of the country, we also felt compelled to do what we could to stand for freedom. With flags and signs in hand, we peacefully protested in Springfield and Milwaukee against an ever-increasing tyrannical overreach of government. I have never appreciated the United States Constitution so much. We were busy meeting with other patriots as well, partly to compare information and partly to strategize how to best protect our families. It was (and is, at publication time) a period of deep media propaganda and uncertainty. Stocking up and planning for an interruption of the flow of goods and/or services became necessary. Again, none of it was conducive to travel.

---

* See *How to Set a Clock at the North Pole*

Then came 2021. Without getting too far into the woods on this one, I will just say that it soared to the top of the list for the worst year since Senator and I had known each other. My beloved mom was diagnosed with cancer in February. In May I developed a strange, extremely painful and debilitating condition that resulted in five months of therapy and appointments. Then out of the blue, with all normal vitals and health statistics, Senator suffered a small stroke in October. Thankfully his recovery was swift and almost 100%. The year closed, however, with the loss of my mom. Yet, God was and is faithful, and I see His hand guiding miraculously on a daily basis. Joy in Him is truly our strength.

Needless to say, 2022 was devoted to pivoting and figuring out our navigation in life rather than in road trips. We planned a fitting and beautiful celebration of life in honor of my mom, spent more time with family, and still incorporated local events. Without intention we became more involved in church, attended a parade, saw fireworks a few times, and even went to several reenactments, stoking our love of history. More challenges came in the autumn, and the country was still on a crazy path (albeit with some improvements), but we were starting to feel a little more hopeful going into 2023.

By the time February rolled around, I was halfway thinking we might be able to manage a short trip. Truth be told, I was nervous. *Me*-- who loved to travel and always had ideas for the next three or four vacations as I was returning from one. I felt almost intimidated by the researching, planning, packing, and execution process. *Should we wait another year?* I wondered. I told Senator my thoughts to get his reaction. He was open to the idea and told me to think about it some more. I was hoping for a more definite answer from him, but as time went on, I started to feel like a trip away together was as necessary as it was desirable. I kept watching for signs that we should not go, but as none came, I found myself relearning my old routines of booking lodging, assembling the necessary notes, and digging out the suitcases. As for the destination, it made sense to pick up where interruptions had left us off, with a trip to Charleston, South Carolina, the prime goal being visiting Fort Sumter.

In true us fashion, there was some atmospheric drama the day before we left. Early spring had seen more than its normal share of tornadic activity in the plains and southern states, and now it was our turn. Northern Illinois was under severe weather warnings, with the potential for hail and/or twisters. We were even sent home early from work so buses could run their routes before the nasty stuff was supposed to hit. In between packing and wrapping things up at home, we monitored live videos of storm trackers in various areas. Thankfully the worst of it missed us, resulting in us getting done with everything we needed to do a few hours earlier than expected. *I'll take it.*

*   *   *

Early on a gray, 40°F Saturday at the beginning of April, we slipped out of the house, out of town, out of the county, and out of the state. The car's stereo was cued up with hours of music we had originally compiled four years ago when we eloped. The clouds, in swirls and swoops of multiple shades of gray, were especially fascinating to me as I drove. Then again, everything looks better when you are exiting Illinois. We kissed as we crossed the state line into Indiana, declaring a victory. *Again, I'll take it.*

North of Indianapolis the sky heaved that vaguely-named 'wintry mix' at us. The winds soon picked up as well, keeping my forearms tense as the steering wheel fought to succumb to the gale from the west. It occurred to me that if the sustained wind ever took a quick break, we would probably be on the shoulder in a split second. It was a little intense, but it was working within the flow of traffic.

Once we were a few miles south of the city, traffic slowed to a crawl. I was actually kind of glad for the break. We assumed another construction zone or perhaps an accident was ahead. Then I looked out the driver side window to see a completely unexpected sight. The guard rail separating the northbound and southbound lanes was covered in large panels of sheet metal. It looked as if a giant had opened sardine cans and discarded the peeled lids to the wind. Soon after, we could see the source of the debris. Out the passenger side window we saw a demolished distribution warehouse. Its remnants reminded me of the Colosseum ruins, with only a partial curved segment remaining. It and a few structures around it had been hit by a tornado the day before. With that knowledge, it was rather impressive that the interstate itself was clear. Though we had driven past tornado destruction once in Kansas, this felt very in-your-face and fresh.

It was about time to stop for gas. We still had plenty, but we allow a generous amount for potential problems. This policy soon justified itself. About five miles past where we saw the destroyed warehouse, we exited. The first station we came to was closed due to not having power. For reasons unknown, they apparently thought it would be more fun to let each carload that stopped learn this fact for themselves, rather than posting a sign to notify people. Upon further inspection, it looked like a few other businesses were also dark, so we got back onto the highway.

We continued a few more miles until we could clearly see lights, and we exited again. This time the first station we came to was fully powered and had a steady line of cars, but it had the distinct disadvantage of not containing any fuel. Fortunately there was another station across the street. This one, too, was busy.

We pulled up to a pump to fill the car and then walked inside to use the bathroom. There was a line of uncomfortable-looking people. For different reasons, some looked just as uncomfortable coming out of the gross restrooms. Let me just say that I was quite masterful at maneuvering through the necessary actions while preventing my person from contacting anything whatsoever. As we reached the car, which was parked in a row at the end of the property, we could see employees starting to cover the pumps. We had bought some of the last gallons of gas they had. "Good thing we stopped when we did," said Senator.

"Yeah, what are they doing? Cutting states off from fuel?" I replied, only halfway joking. After all, we had purposely not listened to any news. Maybe there was a national crisis. Too bad if there was; we were determined to get away on this trip.

After a while we crossed into Kentucky. Almost immediately it was greener, hillier, and distillier. In addition to the signs advertising various purveyors of bourbon, miles of iconic split-rail fences attested to the fact that we were entering horse country. In the midst of it all was a sign for Transylvania University. *Right here in the middle of America... Who knew?*

Just about the time I was losing interest in Kentucky, we crossed into eastern Tennessee. The hills grew higher and eventually reached 'small mountain' status as the billboards beckoned tourists to local attractions and expansive fireworks emporiums. We drove on until it was time to stop for gas again. There was less than an hour until we would be stopping for the day, so if we topped off now, we could get a good start the next day without having to fill up for a while.

We cruised over to the exit ramp and drove to the first station. At this point Senator had been driving. He hopped out the driver side door and looked over the pump as I fished out the credit card. He paused, reading. The machine wasn't working, and we soon realized the handful of other people who had pulled in there were not getting gas either. This station was also sold out. "Should we try another one?" I asked, pointing to a place about half a mile away.

"No, they're not going to have anything, either. Let's just drive a little further." We did, and we successfully filled up long before we were desperate, but it was definitely strange. I suppose it could be related to people trying to avoid or prepare for severe weather the day before. We never really did find out.

About an hour later than my initial plans indicated, we arrived at our hotel. There was a line of a few people at the desk, and the attendant was very friendly with everyone. Friendly is good, but it doesn't move the line along as efficiently as this mover-and-shaker likes to see.* Similar to the rest of the country, this establishment seemed to be short-staffed. That, combined with a phenomenon I had forgotten about known as 'southern time', dragged out the registration process longer than necessary. Longer, but not wrong. This is one of the reasons I like to travel. It reminds me that some of what I consider 'normal' is simply familiar. The two are not necessarily the same.

We had successfully made it through day one. We were on vacation and sleeping in non-Illinois. Beside relaxing, the only other thing on our agenda that night was finding easy food. Next door to the hotel there was a Mexican food chain with which we were unfamiliar. They sold something called a Petro which layered generic Mexican-type ingredients over Fritos. It was hardly health food or home cooked, but there were enough veggies and beans in it to make it solidly acceptable. Done.

*   *   *

The next morning was bright, cool, and just a little misty-- the exact type of morning one desires when one is continuing one's journey through the Smoky Mountains. Being a Sunday, the traffic was light. In fact, being a Sunday in a region where many people still regularly attend church, the initial part of the drive was downright pleasant. Senator adjusted our music as I pulled onto the interstate. I was feeling simultaneously tranquil and enthusiastic as we rose and coasted and curved our way

---

* I have never claimed to be an overly patient person.

around the best roads of the trip.* The change of scenery was good, and by the end of the day, we would be on the Atlantic Coast. I could hardly believe it.

In North Carolina we picked up the heady scent of the clear pine acreage. We both love this smell. I caught it first, as I often do when detecting odors/aromas. A moment or two later Senator picked it up and smiled. We have pine trees near our home, and once it a while the smell of one drifts lightly into the atmosphere, but this was a Christmasy feast for the nose.

The pine forests continued into South Carolina, but the hills did not. Almost at the state border the land became flatter, and somehow it felt like we had entered a deeper level of the South. The weather was warming, but it was not too hot. Still, it just seemed like it would not take much coaxing for the area to envelop its inhabitants in a deep, damp climatic hug. Or maybe Senator and I, who have mutually grown in our detestation of all things hot and humid, were just on guard.

What we really needed to be on guard for, however, where the drivers. Call it a fluke, but we were almost smashed twice due to people who could not merge onto the interstate. It is a skill that simply does not exist in this state.

---

* This trip's road conditions, from best to worst:
1. Tennessee (excellent); 2. North Carolina (very good); 3. Kentucky (good/average); 4. South Carolina (do better); 5. Indiana (holding tight to that Midwest reputation for crappy roads, mitigated only by proximity to Illinois); 6. Illinois (hopeless, recommend selecting alternate route whenever possible... for myriad reasons including excessive potholes; on the plus side, sometimes provides enough busted car parts along city and suburban shoulders for the savvy mechanic to potentially rebuild an entire vehicle)

It is really astounding to glance in the rear view mirror and see a driver who very narrowly missed causing a multiple-car pile up casually enter the desired lane when determined convenient to only himself/herself. Amazing. In retrospect, this could be why every other billboard referenced either God and faith (especially necessary driving here!) or injury attorneys (also valuable to keep in one's contacts).

"Oh, hey," I broke in, once I had relaxed a little from the previous near miss. "Let's put in the Civil War stick drive." On previous journeys to battlefields we had listened to a catalog of old radio shows narrating the scenes as though they had been on site. Senator had somehow stumbled on them via the internet and had downloaded the episodes onto a thumb drive for the car stereo.

"I don't think that's going to work," he replied, examining the drive.

"Why not?" I asked, glad that I at least had not forgotten to pack it.

"It's covered in a sticky goo..."

"Huh?" Other items near it were fine, and nothing had been spilled in the car. Nevertheless, it was now unusable garbage, coated in a brownish muck. "Can they leak, like batteries?" I asked, somewhat intrigued at the thought.

"Apparently they can do something like that."

So much for that plan. I continued driving, shifting my attention to deciphering South Carolina construction signs. "Are these real work zones or not?" The cautious and respectful driver in me tries to adhere to all work zone laws. Likewise, the frugal driver in me would be highly ticked if I got a speeding ticket. The problem was that I could not determine where they started and ended. There were no signs announcing the beginning point of a work zone, and seemingly nothing going on to suggest construction projects, but there were occasional random signs that read, "END ROAD WORK".

"I can't really figure it out either," said Senator.

"Perhaps it's a protest?" I suggested. "Maybe it's not so much that a work zone ends at that spot, as a general airing of grievances at the existence of said road work." Senator conceded the possibility. I chuckled at the thought of angry demonstrators chanting along interstates, waving flags that depicted orange construction cones in circles with slashes through them. A few rowdy ones would get out of hand and try to flip a road grader, quickly learning that it weighed significantly more than your average police car. *We shall o-ver-co-o-ome...*

We arrived in North Charleston ahead of schedule, and Senator was hungry, so we decided to grab a bite to eat and then head to the hotel to check in. The first thing that struck me about the city was that it looked like every known hotel and motel chain in the country was represented. North Charleston was definitely more affordable than the overinflated prices of Charleston accommodations, but I couldn't imagine what would draw so many people to an area that was only on the way to one major city. It seemed like 100,000 people could be housed at our exit alone.

The second thing we could not help but notice were the questionable surroundings. Despite much research and reading endless reviews, the area was not filling us with confidence. I do have to say the Subway 'sandwich artists' were very nice and quite generous with the toppings, but I had my eye on the car the entire time we were in line. Senator wasn't saying much. He didn't need to; I could read his mind.

When we had finished eating, we drove over the interchange toward our hotel. This side was better, but not great. At least if something happened, there would be plenty of witnesses; the area was far more crowded than I had envisioned. I was picturing a typical suburb, but we were in a town that was difficult to read. I can't say anyone was doing anything wrong, exactly, but it sure looked like the potential was there. I also wasn't sure if the signs in our hotel's parking lot made me feel more or less safe. I mean, it was great to know that these premises were "under the jurisdiction of the North Charleston police", but why was it necessary? The lovely palm trees that swayed around the property didn't seem overly concerned.

Inside, the situation was still confusing. The lobby of the reputable chain was clean, modern, and nicely decorated. The desk attendant was also nicely decorated, with comically long nails and a facial piercing that appeared to be a tiny stick pin haphazardly poked into her cheek. On the other hand, she was very friendly as she apologized that our room was not quite ready. "We had a large group check out this morning," she explained. Like everywhere else, they were shorthanded. Senator and I found chairs in the lobby and talked about potential evening plans as we waited. Neither one of us was admitting that we just wanted to see how good or bad the room was before moving too far forward on the agenda.

Thankfully, (and surprisingly, if I am being honest,)

we opened the door to a large, immaculate, quality room that bordered on being a suite. "Oh... well that's good." We could cross that major unknown off the list. I arranged some items in the bathroom and positioned our suitcases for maximum usability over the next three nights. It was satisfying to know I could still zip through these little routines efficiently as though we had not taken an extended hiatus from travel. I felt like myself.

"What's next?" asked Senator.

"Well, there's this tree I was hoping to see..." It sounded like a dumb sentence as I uttered it, but after twenty years Senator has come to expect such conversation openings. "It's the really old oak tree I told you about..." Senator nodded-- remembering or feigning remembering. "Since we have time, I was thinking we could drive down there and see it before we head over to Charleston proper to hang out by the waterfront." Maybe we'd pick up some supper later and watch the sunset oceanside in the historic district. "It's only open until 5:00," I added.

"The waterfront?"

"No, the tree."

"The tree has a closing time?"

"Sort of. There's a road that drives to it, and I think they have a gate or something." (Another in the lengthy list of dumb sentences.)

We were off to view the majestic Angel Oak, exalted by tourists, photographers, and chamber of commerce bigwigs on many a Charleston forum. Unfortunately, the Sunday traffic was discouragingly heavy. No one was going anywhere fast, either on or off the highway. At least it kept moving as we made our way down to Johns Island.* One benefit of the slower pace was that we did not miss noticing the cleverly named flooring store-- Carpet Baggers.

About forty-five minutes after leaving the hotel, we reached a narrow dirt road that ran along a church property and back into a neighborhood. It was about a lane-and-a-half in width and of indeterminant public/private status. Trees shaded most of the drive, and there were crude dirt parking spaces carved out of one side. (It was a good time to be driving a small car.) Like everywhere we had seen since arriving in the greater Charleston area, it was packed. I had expected a handful of serene southerners to be milling about, enjoying the beauty of a massive, old tree. What we saw were dozens of tourists walking their way from their parking spot (gingerly, when a car needed to squeeze by) to the entrance. Most were women in their twenties or thirties, and many were celebrating the warm spring day by sharing a greater vision of themselves than we needed to see.

At the entrance, I had to stop and laugh. The stately 400-year old† live oak was guarded by not just one or two signs asking visitors to be respectful, but an entire ugly, timber-protecting fortress. In case anyone had even a whisper of an abusive thought toward the oak, the land which it occupied, (the size of a few city home lots,) was surrouded by tall metal fencing. To further ensure the

---

* I am fighting the urge to type John's Island, as opposed to Johns Island. I have seen both versions, but the grammatically-disturbing lack of an apostrophe seems to be the preferred and maybe even official spelling. No judgment (or judgement) here, though.

† or 500; sources disagree

tree's safety, barbed wire topped the fence. If you still didn't get the message, multiple signs on the property spelled out the many activities one was specifically *not* permitted to do. Among them was sitting on any part of the tree, whose massive limbs dipped to the ground in several places before swooping back heavenward. Each one on its own was thicker than an average mature oak. Fragile was hardly an image that came to mind. Do not dare to lean yourself or any object against the tree, either. Or get too close to the tree. "Can we breathe on the tree?" I asked Senator. It truly was a magnificent arbor, but the Fort Knox-style overkill detracted significantly from the romance of it. Just in case you want to relive the experience, though, rest assured that the Angel Oak has its own gift shop... also within the confines of its citadel.

While we had been busy *not* touching the Angel Oak, the islands and peninsulas around Charleston had been steadily doubling the amount of cars on the road. Senator was driving, and I was scrambling around Jingles[*] for alternative routes. It did not matter; everywhere was packed. It was not uncommon for us to sit through two or even three cycles of traffic lights while making our way to the historic district. I started to wonder if this is what all cities in states that were growing looked like. After all, people were leaving blue bastions like California, New York, and Illinois like they were on fire.

By the time we eventually reached the waterfront, it was clear that no happy picnics were occurring that evening. Finding parking would require more stamina than we had left, and I wasn't sure where we could even

---

[*] Our G.P.S. sidekick; See *How to Take a Drink From a Cactus*

grab a bite to go. Senator didn't care for the vibe, stating his firm belief that things would change after dark. I can't say I disagreed. We would return the next day for more important stops, and we would see the water up close then.

We returned to North Charleston, never even stopping in Charleston. The evening was disappointing, but I thought perhaps some of the night could be salvaged. Senator spotted a Taco Bell. "Let's just get some food and go back to the hotel." Good enough, except the Taco Bell was out of business, sending us a little further to find something else.

This did not help Senator's mood, which was summoning every negative remembrance he had of the less-than-glamorous aspects of road trips. He ranted a little, took a shower, and went to bed early. I wrestled sad thoughts, read for a while, and eventually settled on a documentary about competing fast food entrepreneurs.[*] The gripping Chick-Fil-A vs. Popeye's suspense sufficed to distract me from a day that ended on a much lower note than it had started. I guess that's all a vegetarian can expect from a show about chicken.

*   *   *

Despite the deflated atmosphere of Sunday night, we actually both got a decent night's sleep. We got ready and enjoyed an excellent, real-food breakfast at the hotel's self-serve buffet, accentuated by Senator's latest companion-- a travel French press for coffee. Today was the main event. For several years we had wanted to see Fort Sumter. We had gone as far as making plans and purchasing tickets in 2020, but the plandemic put it on the back burner. Now I

---

[*] This is a perfect example of why I will never pay for television.

was excited, but I was also nervous that something would go wrong.

It was an ideal morning, though. There was almost no chance of rain, and it was not overly hot.* Through the lobby windows we could see our car in the parking lot. Still there. That's a plus. Maybe the signs worked.

Because it was such a major day in our series of visiting Civil War sites, I had allowed ample time to drive into downtown Charleston, locate the recommended parking deck, and navigate our way to the boat dock. Because we had not been able to scope out the scene the previous evening as intended, I added a little more time. Then, because we had witnessed the outrageous amount of traffic the day before, I backed up our departure time even further. Finally, for general pessimistic purposes, I threw on another fifteen minutes.

All of these considerations proved worthwhile. The traffic was again outrageous. We crept. We waited. We halfway merged. We stopped. We crept some more. We kicked it up to a raging 30mph on the interstate. Soon after, we stopped. In fact, it was comparable to Chicago's traffic, which incorporates far more people, ubiquitous construction projects, and a healthy dose of 'northern aggression'. We did arrive in plenty of time, but we had already mutually vowed to never return to Charleston.†

Both the deck and the dock were easy to find. There were only three other people who were there that early. It gave us time to unwind from the traffic and gaze at the

---

* definitely warmer than the lovely 68°F that the average temperature map had predicted, albeit, but still alright

† It's not like it's on the way to anywhere anyway.

harbor. For some reason I had not even thought about the animal life. Pelicans, other sea birds, and dolphins all put on an impromptu show for us. Huge military and commercial ships dotted the horizon, served by monstrous cranes when docked. The ocean breeze swirled around the coast, keeping us comfortable. We were really going!

The line for boarding began to grow. The boat featured three levels, and it seemed like it held a couple hundred people. I had probably reserved tickets much earlier than I needed to, but it still appeared to be close to sold out. We safely boarded, found seats on the open-air top deck, and listened to instructions and narration during our half-hour sojourn to the island.

There was plenty to see along the way, but my favorite was when we passed Castle Pinckney. Pinckney, which was not a castle but a fort, was a state-of-the-art defense post when it was built around the turn of the century-- the turn of the eighteenth to the nineteenth century, that is. As time and technology progressed, it was outdated by the slick new Fort Sumter in the 1830s. It easily fell into South Carolina's hands after secession, and it was briefly used to house federal prisoners of war. Now Castle Pinckney belongs to the Sons of Confederate Veterans, as the flag over it attests. There are no stars and stripes flying over Pinckney; the Bonnie Blue proudly and stubbornly waves over its defiant fortification.[*]

Before long, Fort Sumter came into view. Its dark-brown brick walls surrounded it staunchly, though now considerably shorter than during the War Between the

---

* medium/dark blue background with a single, white five-pointed star at the center

States. At the moment, the enormous flagpole was bare. We docked, disembarked, and walked inside onto a grassy field.

In December 1860, when it became clear that South Carolina no longer considered itself part of the United States of America, federal troops under Major Robert Anderson evacuated Fort Moultrie secretly during the night, moving operations to Fort Sumter, which was better positioned to defend against not only foreign invaders from the sea, but hostile forces within Charleston. A month later Anderson was running low on supplies and could use more men, so the federal government sent a supply ship to him, treating the area as part of the United States, as they always had. This did not play well with the locals. South Carolina troops fired on *Star of the West*, sending it skedaddling back northward.

In March, tensions were further elevated when Confederate States of America President Jefferson Davis appointed Brigadier General P.G.T. Beauregard to head Charleston forces. In early April, United States of America President Abraham Lincoln notified the Confederacy that he fully intended to send reinforcements to Anderson at Sumter. That was the final straw for Davis and the Confederacy. They considered Lincoln's nonrecognition of their believed sovereignty as an act of war and responded accordingly. On April 12, 1861, Beauregard's troops attacked Fort Sumter, sparking what some considered a second American war for independence, and what others considered an illegitimate rebellion.

Around the inside of the perimeter we saw cannon still positioned for defense, some on half-circle tracks for maneuverability. A few holes remained, but they were boarded up. Inner walls formed the outlines of powder magazines and other storage rooms. An upper level of the fort featured a very small museum, whose crown jewels are two flags. One is Major Robert Anderson's United States flag, which actually flew over Fort Sumter during the 1861 bombardment. The other is an early version of South Carolina's palmetto flag, the first flag to be raised over the fort in 1861.

During the crossing to the island, our park ranger had mentioned the possibility of assisting with the raising of the flag. I had read such rumors online, claiming that the raising only occurred during the first tour of the day. Naturally, this solidified my choice of tour time, just in case the chance arose. Once these facts were confirmed, as you can imagine, I determined to step up and volunteer, though I usually hate to be in the spotlight. It was too cool an opportunity to pass up.

When the magical moment arrived and the ranger called for any volunteers, I was just about ready to stage my siege, (especially since there were so many more people on the tour than I was expecting,) when I was stymied. A bunch of eager kids made their way to the base of the flagpole. I had not planned for that situation. My conscience kicked in, along with a flood of memories of all the wonderful experiences my parents had exposed me to at various historical sites while on family vacations. I stopped, yielding the honor to persons shorter than myself. After all, it was a blessed thing to witness children who still cared about history and our country.

The group got situated as I consoled my mild

disappointment, half-grinning toward Senator, who had already read my mind. Then something wonderful happened. The park ranger graciously praised the many youth volunteers, but also asked for "a few adult volunteers to join us". That was my cue. I made a bee line for the flagpole, employing a steely forward gaze that precluded any eye contact which would suggest deference to others. Kids I would step aside for; other adults, no way.

History Wendy was in position. My hands were tightly gripping my assigned portion of the massive, heavy cloth of the pristine United States flag. My feet were firmly planted, lest I get raised with it. My favorite "Live Free or Die" shirt proudly announced my patriotic sentiment. Last but not least, my sunglasses conveniently hid my eyes, which were tearing up faster than I could process. Not that I wasn't smiling; I was beaming. There were just so many aspects of history and strife and patriotism and heartbreak and division and beginnings and endings and victory and reunification and repeated cycles and lingering constitutional questions associated with this curious war. It all felt concentrated at that point. I knew it would be a memorable and meaningful moment, but I did not know how intensely moving it would be.

Smiling and subtly sniffling my way back toward where Senator was standing, I was very satisfied. He was enjoying himself, too, finally settling into being able to focus on the objective of the trip. We concluded our time on the island with a walk around the quiet sandbar. Turning to face various directions, we mentally established the geography of the harbor and the locations of the attack. The puzzle was fitting together in a way no book or map could convey.

Back on land we made a quick stop at the visitor center. It was very crowded with the next batch of passengers, but we took a few minutes to glance around the displays. Most of the information was familiar, but I did learn that long before cotton was king, rice reigned. Initially it accounted for more agricultural production than any of the other southern staples like tobacco or sugar.

Though our next stop was within moderate walking distance, we decided to leave the parking deck and find a closer spot. We did not fully trust the local vibe, and we were not sure about access crossing busier streets. Not walking too far also guaranteed it would not rain. Thankfully, we were blessed with a perfect spot on a side street with plenty of tourist foot traffic. Unlike Chicago, parking rates for the day remained in the single digits.

From the car it was about two blocks west to the Powder Magazine. We wound down a short garden path to an obscure entrance where a guide waved us in. My first impression was that it was very cozy, which was probably not the primary intention of the designer. The wood floor creaked as we paid our admission and received some basic information. Senator was drawn to a few books for sale on a nearby shelf.

The building's claim to fame is that it is the oldest public building in the Carolinas, dating back to the early 1700s. As harbor activity and the city grew, it was determined that a safe place was needed to house the highly explosive commodity of gunpowder. As one diarist from the period observed, "If God should decide to strike [Charleston] with lightning, it would take half the town with it!" Though only the size of a small, single-story home, its three-foot thick walls and criss-cross peaked roof lines protected tons of gunpowder. Should tragedy occur and the powder ignite, sand in the attic would, in theory, rain down on the explosion and help quell the blast.

"This part," our ranger explained, "has not been tested."

We perused the exhibits along the walls. Many related to the area's colonial history, especially as it applied to trade. Pirates also played a prominent role in the harbor, leaving their own imprint on the economy of the time. The most interesting tidbit I picked up about South Carolina's eighteenth century history was the date that it declared independence from Britain-- *March* 1776. These people don't wait around for freedom!

We walked back to the car, past a beautiful old Anglican church. In fact, Charleston's nickname is the 'Holy City', due to all of the churches. Right across the street, however, were a few dumpy buildings that looked like they had been abandoned for some time. It was a strange city to figure.

After a brief map consultation, we learned that our next stop was close enough to walk, so we left the car and turned south. Several blocks later we turned toward the entrance of the Old Slave Mart. Understandably, one might wonder about a museum housed in the surviving building of a complex built to advertize and sell humans. (In fact, the museum was once the showroom.) This museum, though, was presented extremely well, with accurate perspectives from many people's firsthand experiences. The caretakers worked hard to go beyond the one-dimensional picture presented in most educational settings. For example, most people don't know that some slaves were very highly skilled, making great contributions in areas ranging from carpentry to ship piloting to blacksmithing. Agriculture was only one realm of their labor. Politically-ignored information was incorporated as well, like the fact that some free black people owned black slaves.

Other exhibits went into depth on the trasportation conditions of ships that carried slaves across the Atlantic Ocean. Shackles from the period were on display as a very real reminder of the limits of forced servitude. Personal narratives also told how slaves were coached on how to answer probing questions from perspective buyers. Tricks were employed to make labor appear younger, healthier, or better skilled than they were, all in the name of profit. Overall, it was a fascinating stop that measured up to its reputation for accuracy and excellence.

Covering two centuries of history made us hungry, so we returned to the car to determine our options. Something more substantial than granola bars was called for, moving our attention to the buzzing block to the north of us. We fed the meter another monetary snack and proceeded on foot. "I guess our parking spot was even better than we realized," I remarked.

We did not want to waste time sitting down, so the best alternative appeared to be a New York City-style pizza-by-the-slice joint. Not very Charleston, but enticing enough to meet the demand. Perhaps they did maintain a nod to their southern location, as the service was s...l...o...w. It was an odd juxtaposition to the loud heavy metal playing on the speakers, the crowded line, the young child screaming in one of the few booths, and the thickly-makeuped, no-nonsense Bronxy broad managing all of the orders. In the end, our subpar pizza was portable enough to eat on the street and decent enough to fuel us for the afternoon ahead.

From our car's pivot point we headed east a few blocks to the waterfront. We soon approached the park I had originally planned to visit the night before, when I was a young, naive girl who thought one could enjoy a quiet harborside evening in Charleston. The iconic pineapple fountain emerged in our view, raining water down its prickly and spiky architecture to a few delighted children below. There were lots of people at the park and around the fountain, but we had no more expectations of semi-private walks. A quick photo by the fountain, another of Castle Pinckney to the east, and a walk under the intertwined archway of gnarly trees met all of our waterfront needs.

This time we stayed in the car when we went back to it. Our spot had served us well for exploration in all four cardinal directions. Now I just wanted one quick spin past the mansions of the French Quarter and we could call it a day.[*] Senator fired up Jingles, and I watched for oblivious pedestrians as we pulled out.

This is the Charleston everyone knows-- colonial French and Spanish architecture painted in pastels and deep, soft hues. It's a place, at least in this neighborhood,

---

[*] I say 'mansions', but in reality, these were small palaces, arranged with fancy columns and scrollwork on multiple levels, giving them the appearance of exquisitely-frosted layer cakes.

where you could paint your home coral or sky blue, and no one would question your vision. As impressively wide as the homes are, they go back three times as long to the rear. Gardens and chains of ivy squeeze their way between properties, accenting iron gates that keep the wandering bachelorette partiers and overly curious tourists at bay. Nearby Rainbow Row flaunts its tasteful colorful variations for every magazine photographer who ever stepped foot in the American Holy City. For our purposes, all of it could be sufficiently enjoyed within a mile or two, from the car, on our way out of Charleston.

"Something I will never comprehend," I mused, "is why, if a person had so much money he could afford a humungous house like that, he would not buy land to go with it. Who wants to be right next to your neighbors? Some of these people could shake hands out their windows!" Senator offered his theories:

1.) People this wealthy have several homes, so they don't mind being close to their neighbors (whom they have likely never met) for a few days here and there. *Ah, makes sense.*
2.) These are people who want to *be seen* as much as they want to see the views of the harbor. *Can't relate.*
3.) Some people thrive on the activity of lots of human interaction. They want to step out their front door, descend their palatial staircase, and enter the action. *Definitely can't relate.*

Before leaving the historic district we made a pass by The Battery. This southern tip of the peninsula curves along the harbor in the form of a very green military park.

Gnarly oaks shaded statues of men like Colonel William Moultrie, the antagonist of Fort Sumter. Cannon were positioned throughout the grounds, and Spanish moss accented the lovely scene. Plenty of people were enjoying the park, but we were ready to head back to the hotel.

Again our preferred night life was a quick stop to pick up some food, followed by relaxing in our room. We had packed a lot into the day. I cleaned up and plopped down on the bed, notebook and pen in hand to jot down details of what we had seen and done. We each took turns recalling different moments that had made an impact on us. Of course, for me, the highlight was the flag raising over Fort Sumter. Mission accomplished.

* * *

Tuesday we had another full agenda. Though we left in what should have been plenty of time to reach our first destination when expected, the traffic was worse than the previous two days combined. At least the places we were going today did not have any specifically timed tickets associated with them. Along the way we passed two cemeteries that were visible from points on the interstate. "They're probably all the people who died while waiting to exit I-26..." I commented. It was ridiculous, and definitely contained a higher road-misery factor than Chicago, which, as I have alluded to, is saying a lot.

What should have taken a little less than half an hour took a full hour and a half. At least the views of the harbor from the elevated highway to Mount Pleasant were pleasant.[*] We eventually cruised into a yuppie seacoast

---

[*] Although, by my rough count, the number of mounts on the Mount Pleasant peninsula is approximately zero.

haven of vacation homes and the kinds of restaurants and shops that exist for the kinds of people who pretty much do the same things on vacation that they do when they are home. There is nothing wrong with that, but we were happy to get past the upper crust to the marshy areas of Sullivan's Island.

Here, tucked in the depths of an expensive neighborhood, was Fort Moultrie. Originally constructed of palmetto logs and sand, Fort Moultrie served the United States in various defense capacities from the 1770s through World War II. In fact, the iconic palmetto tree on South Carolina's flag honors the fort's effectiveness against a British naval attack in 1776. As it turns out, palmetto is dense and relatively squishy, making it an excellent material for a primitive fort.

The fort's best-known intersection with history, however, was its role in the months and days leading up to the War Between the States. In December 1860, South Carolina became the first state to formally secede from the Union. Major Robert Anderson, commander of Fort Moultrie, quickly realized that bordering the properties of residents who considered 1.)themselves South Carolinians, 2.)the United States a hostile foreign country, and 3.)Mr. Lincoln a tyrant, was not the best position in which to find one's small military unit. Thus, he stealthily scooted out to the aquatically-surrounded Fort Sumter, leaving Moultrie vacant. Though evacuation was a wise move, it merely bought time until Sumter was attacked. Naturally, Fort Moultrie, now occupied by South Carolina forces, was used as the prime point of bombardment against Fort Sumter, kicking off the war everyone but the most naive knew was inevitable. Unlike his evacuation from Fort Moultrie, Anderson's evacuation from Sumter was not voluntary.

It was getting hot quickly as we parked and walked into the visitor center. The sun was very bright, and it took a minute to adjust to the lower light inside. I then noticed the sign behind the desk. The entry fee of twenty bucks was decidedly *un*pleasant, but we wanted to see it, and I reasoned that inflation was so bad it wasn't really like dropping a Jackson. I paid our admission, and we entered the small theatre, where the interpretive film was about to start.

The short movie covered a useful overview of the fort's service during its long tenure. Senator thought the presentation was cheesy, and he was not wrong, but it helped me connect the dots and understand the changing defense needs of the growing country. It was amazing to think that the fort started with cannon and retired with radio technology. I wondered what it would be like if it were still being used today.

After the film we wandered around the exhibit room, where we learned more interesting facts related to the fort. For example, did you know, Reader, that a German U-boat was sunk outside Charleston Harbor?[*] Mines and submarine nets were as real off the South Carolina coast as they were around Europe or the United Kingdom. What if Axis forces had made it ashore?

The rear doors of the visitor center opened to a street that one simply had to cross to be on the old fort's footprint. (It was easy to see why Anderson had felt threatened.) We walked into the enclosure of the fort along a circular path

---

[*] Not recently; don't worry.

that took us through the fort's various iterations. Each section was dedicated and restored to a different period in its history: Colonial era, War of 1812, World War I, and World War II. Very large atillery was present, and there were a few levels of embankments with underground tunnels leading to storage or office spaces. The echo in those places was incredible.

Back outside we climbed one section for a beautiful view of Fort Sumter. It was bright and hot, but the water looked peaceful and inviting. Senator performed his long-honed art of posing me, setting the timer, and running to join me in just enough time to beat the *click* of the camera. This ritual solidified the fact that we were back on vacation.

One thing I noticed while driving (or sitting in traffic) in South Carolina was the pride the residents had in their state. We have traveled to every state and province, and nowhere beats South Carolina for the percent of people flying their state flag. Maybe this is more of a Charleston thing, but a noticeable percent of the homes and businesses waved their palmetto. What was even more telling was that only about half of the places which flew the state flag also flew the U.S. flag. This is almost never the case in other places. In Illinois, it would be downright laughable for anyone to fly the state flag without an American flag somewhere above it attempting to mitigate the embarrassment. Usually public buildings are the only ones who willingly admit their association with the failing and corrupt state. You couldn't pay me to fly one!*

The next leg of our drive moved along much better than the morning had, but it was still crowded. When we

---

* unless it was upside-down

arrived at Boone Hall Plantation, we were only fifteen minutes later than I was hoping. Boone Hall holds the distinction of being one of the oldest operating farms in North America. Like Fort Moultrie, it has witnessed many changes in the nation's history.

We entered the property through the famous Avenue of Oaks, which is exactly what you are picturing. If you don't know what I mean, pick up any cheap romance novel and look at the background of the cover photo. Two neatly arranged parallel rows of formidable live oaks greet you graciously while reminding you that they were here long before you were. Supposedly it is the most photographed plantation in America. I can believe it.

Once we found parking in the overflow lot, we hoofed our way to the small information building, where we were assured that it was imperative to claim our house tour time. "Okay, what's available?" I inquired.

"1:45!" replied the friendly man behind the desk, as though I had made his day by asking. He then produced his official purple marker and plastered the time on a schedule for us.

"Thank you!" we told him. I scanned the events, the locations, and the times, scribbling a master plan in the margin.

"I'm following *you*," said Senator. It is his usual code for telling me he's up for whatever I want to do or see, so long as it does not require too much planning on his part.

A presentation was just about to begin near the slave cabins. Unlike most plantation sites, Boone Hall has nine surviving cabins, each with fireplace and windows on two sides. Whereas most quarters were made of wood, Boone

Hall produced bricks on the property, creating stronger cabins. Better preserved structures take some of the guesswork out of understanding the daily life of enslaved people.

We took a break from exploring the buildings to listen to a presentation by one of the guides. He explained that one of the biggest challenges for slaves at Boone Hall was finding good water. Coastal areas have saltwater, of course. Other sources were brackish, and wells were not an option. Thus, the best source of water was collecting rain water.

He went on to discuss the daily lives and duties at the plantation, which included a lot of food production and preparation. Apparently one local enslaved woman gained a reputation as a legendary cook. I believe a descendant of hers even opened a restaurant. Faith and shared stories were also part of the culture.

One visitor asked where slaves were buried. It was a good question; I had never heard of formal graveyards on plantation properties. The guide's response was, "Much of Charleston is built on unmarked graves." He explained that it was a regular occurrence for a construction project to halt due to finding human remains.

We cut out from that presentation a little early to catch another talk. This one was given by a reenactor who was a descendant of lowcountry Gullah people. Immediately the dialect fascinated me. It was very fast and very Caribbean, yet different from the Jamaicans or Haitians I have heard. Her accent was pure Gullah, whereas it was diluted further up the coast or further inland. In addition to speaking, she sang. It was a fitting rendition of the prayers and codes used to communicate hope or a chance for freedom.

It was about 1:30, and our schedule clearly beamed our 1:45 tour time, so we made our way to the house. It was large, but not what I would call a mansion. Its best feature was the two-story columned porch with its rocking chairs perched in the shade. Senator claimed one, but not before we were asked if, indeed, we were 1:45ers. I produced our handwritten purple proof, which satisfied the guide. Evidently there is a seedy underworld of tourists trying to infiltrate tour times to which they have not been granted permission.

Interestingly, the home has been continually occupied by one family or another since its construction. Unfortunately, this leaves most of it closed off from the public, even when they are on the correct tour. We did get to see an elaborate dining room, entry hall, library, and garden loggia, though. The libary sported two pianos, neither of which we were allowed to touch.[*]

We exited the home and circled around through the formal gardens, whose paths formed the lines of butterfly wings. Ahead lay the end of the Avenue of Oaks, so we took another picture. Had it not been so hot and sticky, it might have been funny to duplicate a romance book cover, but my capri jeans and tee shirt would not have worked too well. Senator does sort of have the right hair, though...

Hot it was. The temperature hung around 85°F plus plenty of humidity. It was a far cry from the comfortable highs they usually experienced this time of year. I know

---

[*] The guide was polite about the rules, though. The Angel Oak owners could take a lesson or two.

people adapt and their bodies get used to climates, but there is no way Senator and I could ever live in the South. Northern Illinois summers are miserable enough, and we are generally sick of them by the end of May.

We ducked into the store to buy more water. They were also selling luscious strawberries that were harvested on the property, but there were too many in each container. We did not want to waste them, and they never would have survived in the heat. On the other hand, Senator could not resist boiled, salted, in-shell peanuts. They were the perfect snack for a sweaty South Carolina afternoon. Unlike the ones occasionally sold at home, they were soft enough to chew and digest. The ones I had tried before always left me choking on what felt like shards of wood.

We were a little early for our last activity of the day, but we walked over to the departure point of the farm and nature tour, since there were shaded benches where we could wait. As it turned out, the previous tour was leaving a little later than anticipated, and they had exactly two seats (together) left on the wagon. Senator casually stepped up, still nibbling his peanuts, and assisted me. A moment later we were riding along, catching a light breeze as our covered tram was pulled by the tractor.

I thought it would be a nice little ride around the grounds, but it was more informative and impressive than I was picturing. In the midwest, such a ride circles around the outskirts of zillions of rows of corn, possibly interrupted by half-a-zillion rows of soybeans. If the ride occurs in October, pumpkins will be the focus instead. That's about all the variety you can hope for. Here, our tour wound around through woods, marsh, and fields, ranging from thick vegetation to airy open spaces. Dozens of different vegetables and types of fruit were grown.

There were also bee hives, and a smaller version of a once-extensive orchard. Some time ago a hurricane had taken out thousands of the trees, yet only two live oaks had been lost. Our guide explained that this was due to the complex intertwining of their root systems underground, and the small leaves on spread-out branches that allow the winds to flow through freely. Thus, the stately Avenue of Oaks stands strong.

Wildlife was abundant, including turtles, birds, and small critters. There was even a deer and an eagle's nest, which I do not associate with the South. The alligator in the pond kept his eyes fixated on our group, however, confirming our latitude. Our guide informed us that there was also a considerable snake population, including a few poisonous varieties, in the denser parts of the property-- *no thanks*!

Capping it all off were the clearly visible trenches dug in the woods of one part of the property's far reaches. We had seen Civil War earthworks built by soldiers in Virginia and Tennessee, but this was different. As the war moved into the region, owners thought it prudent to create a barrier to dissuade Yankee forces from coming up to ransack the land and home. It may have been effective; any Yankees who invade now have to pay admission.

It was time to go. Within just miles of the estate we were back in the twenty-first century and back in its maddening traffic. It was a little bit startling. Inside the 700+ acres of Boone Hall Plantation you would never know all of this exists. You don't see it or hear it. You barely remember it, until the oaks are far out of view.

For months we had been carrying around a Trader Joe's* gift card, generously given to us by a family member. We do not live near any of the chain's locations, so I had the bright idea to bring it with us on vacation. When I planned our route, I learned we would be near one of their stores in Mount Pleasant. I had envioned picking up some frozen dinner items to take back to our hotel room, where there was a fridge and microwave. The hot weather and the recently-acquired knowledge that the commute back would take much longer than it should scrapped this plan. Instead, we coexisted with the local yuppies just long enough to grab some nonperishable snacks for the ride home.

We were hot and tired. Once again our room had not been visited by any housekeeping staff. We didn't need our bed made, but fresh towels were needed, and the tiny garbage can was full once we added more used carryout containers. Apparently the little cards that you used to leave out if you didn't want the room made up no longer apply. Now hotels and motels everywhere assume this as the default position. This is fine, except no one tells you. By the time we checked out the next day, we had quite the collection of used towels on the bathroom floor.

As we relaxed, Senator saw that bad storms were predicted for Frankfort, Kentucky, where we would be staying the next night. We consulted several radars and hourly forecasts and determined that our current timeline was still probably best. It was a tentative situation, though.

---

* not to be confused with Traitor Joe, the fool occupying the White House at press time

We decided to reassess in the morning, setting the alarm early. If necessary, we could leave earlier or later. In the meantime, we agreed to switch over to watching comedy rather than weather.

*   *   *

At 6:00am the alarm started blaring. We stumbled our way over to the computer and checked all of the same sources we had viewed the night before. According to them, the severe weather was still on the same predicted track. There was no point in leaving early; that would have placed us smack-dab in the middle of it upon our arrival. We lay back down for an hour and then got ready to go. Accounting for heavy traffic, we should arrive after things had shifted to rain only.

Leaving South Carolina did not make us sad. It had been a great trip history-wise, but we were out of place. Just as we crossed into North Carolina, low mountains came into view. Low mountains, that is, and a major construction project. Parallel to our side of the interstate was the longest continuous road project I had ever seen. An unbroken chain of gutted land, industrial vehicles, and workers painted the landscape orange for dozens and dozens of miles.

The construction eventually tapered off, but the traffic never did. In parts of eastern Tennessee we got a very good view of the Smokies, as we were completely stopped. The heat radiated off of the side of the hills, bouncing the sun's rays around us to produce a stagnant 92°F. I will gladly bring up this fact the next time an Illinoisan tells me to move to Tennessee, where, he or she claims, the summers aren't that bad in the mountainous

37

parts. This was the first week of April; I sure wouldn't want to stick around for July.*

We managed to avoid the storms until the last twenty minutes of our drive. The radars had been remarkably accurate. Nearing Frankfort we could see menacing clouds swirling. At least traffic had been reasonable throughout the Kentucky portion of our drive. On the horizon we could see a distinct white curtain of heavy rain. We drove forward into it, but we did not encounter any lightning or hail. Traffic slowed to a steady 45mph, but we could still see well enough.

To make matters more interesting, Jingles took us on a convoluted route to our hotel. It did not match what I had written down, but it landed in the same place at the same projected time, so we stuck with it. Senator did raise an eyebrow when Jingles told us to turn down Martin Luther King Drive. In every city I've been to, that is not a place that warmly welcomes out-of-towners. This one, however, showed no signs of trouble.

In the pouring rain we reached our hotel. It was a large, ugly cement structure that looked like an office building designed to suck the life out of reluctant cogs in a cubicle machine. The interior, on the other hand, was clean and green. A large rambling lobby was modern but not severe, incorporating lanterns, many plants, and a wall waterfall. Most walls were decorated with something related to Kentucky State University, whose campus it bordered.

---

* To be fair, we later learned that part of the heat wave was driven by the same storm system we were trying to avoid-- one that spawned more tornadoes in Illinois and Missouri.

The personnel situation was unusual as well. The only people we saw passing through the lobby were groups of two or three, mostly men, and definitely younger and more in shape than us. This put us on our guard, but most went out of their way to say "Hello" or wish us a good evening. They appreared to be connected to the college, though it seemed strange that they were in a private hotel. I was starting to wonder whether I had misunderstood my reservation.*

The woman at the front desk was the only person around who looked like a typical hotel staff member or patron. She appeared overjoyed to see us. I wasn't sure how to take that. I could sense Senator trying to decipher the situation. "Welcome!!" the woman began. I gave her my name. "I see through our reservation service that you are a V.I.P.! That means we have some gifts for you!" She presented us with a hearty bag of snacks and literature about the city.

Senator looked over at me, surprised that I had been keeping my illustrious status a secret. I shrugged. "Guess you're lucky to be with me," I muttered. We took our key as the woman explained the parking situation.

Crap-- deck parking. I had somehow missed this detail when booking. At this point we had no better option, so we drove next door to the deck, parked in as illuminated spot as possible, as near the exit as possible. I prayed over the car, kept my 'equalizer' handy, and did my best to ignore the graffiti on the far side of the parking deck.

We dodged our way through the downpour back to the hotel entrance. A few more young guys entered as well.

---

* Maybe I had just enrolled us for a semester!

39

They took the same elevator as us, telling us to have a good night as they exited to their floor. My theory is that the university needed more student housing, and the old hotel could no longer fill the hundreds of rooms they had, now that chains dotted the interstate exits, so they worked out a deal. I just hoped this did not mean our room would look like a disgusting dorm.

Two floors up we stepped out of the elevator. I had to laugh as we popped the key card into the door. "What's so funny?" asked Senator.

"Of course we're in room 420," I answered. "What's more appropriate for our unintentional foray into college land?"

The room was actually very nice, and the bathroom was fancier than most places we stay. Everything was in working order and clean, and the television was better than ours at home. I put it to good use just before we left on a pizza run. "What are you doing?" asked Senator, as I selected the ESPN channel and turned the volume up a little louder than normal listening level.

"Just in case these kids aren't all here for the academics, I want it to sound like someone's in our room... preferably someone young and male."

"Good idea." *Man, growing up in Joliet has ruined us.*

Our car had survived its first absence from us. We drove it to a pizza place a few miles away and collected our box of hot supper to take back to the room. Once again we parked as strategically as possible. I still halfway expected the car to be gone in the morning. One more prayer couldn't hurt. On the plus side, I did notice that every other vehicle in the deck was better than ours, including one that two students (I hope) got out of.

*   *   *

Thursday morning I awoke to the sound of sirens. We were on a major street, so I didn't really pay attention at first. Then more came along, so I figured I should see what was up, in case the hotel was on fire or something. I pulled the heavy drape back a little, blinding myself for a second. When I refocused, I could see emergency vehicles speeding down the road. *Okay, it's not us.* I glanced at the clock. We probably would have been up soon anyway, so we started to get ready. The big question in my mind was the car.

Before leaving we took the elevator down to the lobby to scope out the breakfast situation. The desk attendant had given me two little paper ticket vouchers, but we had not noticed any obvious eating area when we had checked in. "Oh, I think I see a sign," I said. At the rear of the lobby a short hallway opened up to a large banquet room. We entered, glancing around to get the lay of the land.

A sign firmly reminded students that breakfast was for hotel patrons only, and that they were to eat on campus in the cafeteria. I guess my student housing theory was right. A few friendly servers stood around, smiling and waiting for anything that needed replenishing. They greeted us and directed me to drop our tickets into a basket. Senator and I selected a table by the window to watch the quiet, gray morning as we ate. And eat we did. Multiple breakfast items were arranged at different stations. I am not a breakfast person, but I do indulge on vacation. At least if we had to walk the rest of the way home, we were going on a full stomach.

After eating we sipped our coffee for a few more minutes before making a motion to leave. I'm never a fan of this part of traveling. There's nothing else to see except ugly road, so I just want to click my heels and be home in an instant. Having no ruby slippers, however, we wrapped up, got our gear, and checked out. The last thing I saw before leaving the hotel was a giant banner I had somehow missed. It read "Thank You for Voting Us #1 Hotel in Frankfort!" *Hhmmm...*

It was pouring, and Senator insisted on getting the car to pull up. "Don't you think we should go together?" I asked, (strength in numbers and such).

"No, it's fine. You wait here with our stuff."

I was very pleased to see both him and our car arrive a few minutes later. We are not paranoid people. We are not even pessimistic people. We have just spent too much time in cities where attitude, entitlement, and violence are the norm. I don't know if we qualify as 'street smart', but we sure make it a point to be on guard. We will continue to do this, but it was nice to know it wasn't wholly necessary.

Our trip continued in the rain, into Indiana. Senator was driving, declaring his traditional last-day promise of, "*I'll* get us home." Translation: "I will drive us safely but swiftly, and come hell or high water, we will be sleeping in our own bed tonight!" I appreciated this commitment, as traffic was soon very heavy again, and we saw more than our share of crazy drivers. We are both starting to think that maybe self-driving cars would not be such a bad thing. Sure, there would be a few mishaps here and there, but on average, would they be any worse than what we have been witnessing on the roads lately? Who knows? Maybe we'll find out on some future trip...

Afterword

I want to sincerely thank everyone who has read any or all of this series.

If you are someone who travels, you are probably doing it better than us. Still, I hope you have found a few interesting or entertaining bits in our tales. Maybe you have written or will write your own stories. (Trust me, they are more intriguing than you realize.)

If you are someone who used to travel but is no longer able to, I hope this has kindled your own fond memories. Dust off those old photos or videos if you have them.

If you are someone who has always wanted to travel, but who has been intimidated by the process, I hope you have been inspired to give it a shot. (No, it won't go perfectly-- it might even have you swearing at me halfway through the trip-- but you will gain an invaluable experience.)

If you are someone who has zero interest in traveling, I hope our adventures (good and bad) have made you appreciate your armchair and your home. Kick off your shoes and enjoy.

If you are my Essential Other, I can never sufficiently thank you for being brave enough, inconvenienced enough, resilient enough, fun enough, and loving enough to run around with me and share these journeys. As I told you in 2003, "I really like hanging around with you, Senator."

~Wendy V
May 2023

Space for Your Own Travel Notes...

www.ingramcontent.com/pod-product-compliance
Lightning Source LLC
Chambersburg PA
CBHW031657040426
42453CB00006B/329